W9-AZM-539

THE HUMAN BODY IN 3D

THE LUNGS IN 3D

rosen publishing's
rosen central

HOPE LOURIE KILLCOYNE
AND CHRIS HAYHURST

For Ronald Chodosh, MD, one of the finest and most dedicated pulmonologists ever—and a great dad, too

Published in 2016 by The Rosen Publishing Group, Inc.
29 East 21st Street, New York, NY 10010

Copyright 2016 by The Rosen Publishing Group, Inc.

First Edition

Library of Congress Cataloging-in-Publication Data

Killcoyne, Hope Lourie.
The lungs in 3D/Hope Lourie Killcoyne and Chris Hayhurst.
    pages cm.—(The human body in 3D)
Includes bibliographical references and index.
ISBN 978-1-4994-3605-1 (library bound)—ISBN 978-1-4994-3606-8 (pbk.)—
ISBN 978-1-4994-3608-2 (6-pack)
1. Lungs—Juvenile literature. 2. Respiration—Juvenile literature. I. Hayhurst, Chris. II. Title.
QP121.K54 2016
611'.24—dc23

3 1907 00355 0307

2015000140

Manufactured in the United States of America

CONTENTS

INTRODUCTION

In 1961, as a twenty-five-year-old medical student at the University of Basel in Switzerland, Ronald Chodosh, born and raised in the Bronx, New York, had a startling moment during his first autopsy, which he performed on an elderly Swiss man. The lungs of this near-ninety-year-old, who had spent his entire life in the hills of the Swiss countryside, were a lovely shade of pink. Not surprising, you say? That's how lungs are depicted in images everywhere—from television to the Internet to the illustrations within these very pages. That is true. But in *real* life, lungs don't stay pink for long. In the autopsies Chodosh had observed back in New York City, lungs—even those of young people—were, at best, gray, beige, or brown. And those of smokers

Connecting the throat to the lungs is a large tube called the windpipe. Also known as the trachea, it brings air in and out of the lungs through the two bronchi, which themselves lead to the branchlike bronchioles.

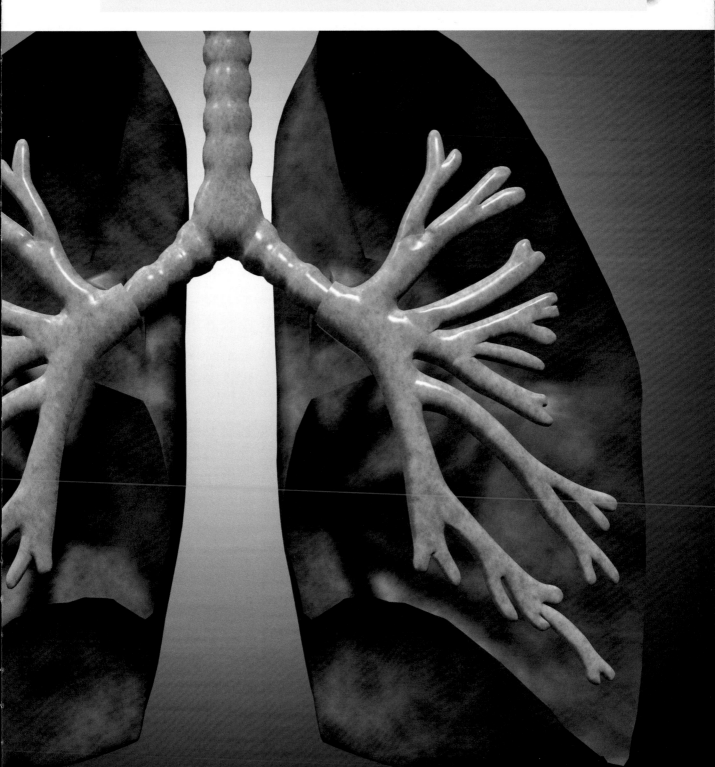

were far darker, with patches of a blackish charcoal color scattered about.

Lungs are indeed our sponges, filtering the air we breathe. If you live in the grassy valleys of Switzerland's Alps, there's a good chance that your lungs are rosier than if you live in the smog-filled industrial city of Norilsk, Russia, which has been declared as being one of the most polluted places on earth. Have you ever looked at the filter of an air-conditioning unit? Our lungs are kind of like that, but they're *dynamic*, actually enabling us to breathe. And they're working all the time, whether you're paying attention (such as during a game of soccer) or not (such as when you read—except, of course, for when you read a resource such as this that calls your attention to an involuntary bodily function). And how many times does the average teenager breathe in an hour? At rest, it's around 1,200 times. That's right: over a thousand times. And you're not even paying attention. Usually.

Of course, there are people who are *always* paying attention to their breathing—people who have respiratory problems, such as asthma. Ronald Chodosh himself was one such person. In 1944, when he was eight years old, the latest remedy of the day for such a disorder—said remedy based at a clinic in Biloxi, Mississippi—was treatment with arsenic, a chemical now recognized as being poisonous and thus a main ingredient in many insecticides. Live and learn. Happily, Ronald Chodosh lived long past the "treatment," going on to become an expert and empathic pulmonologist,

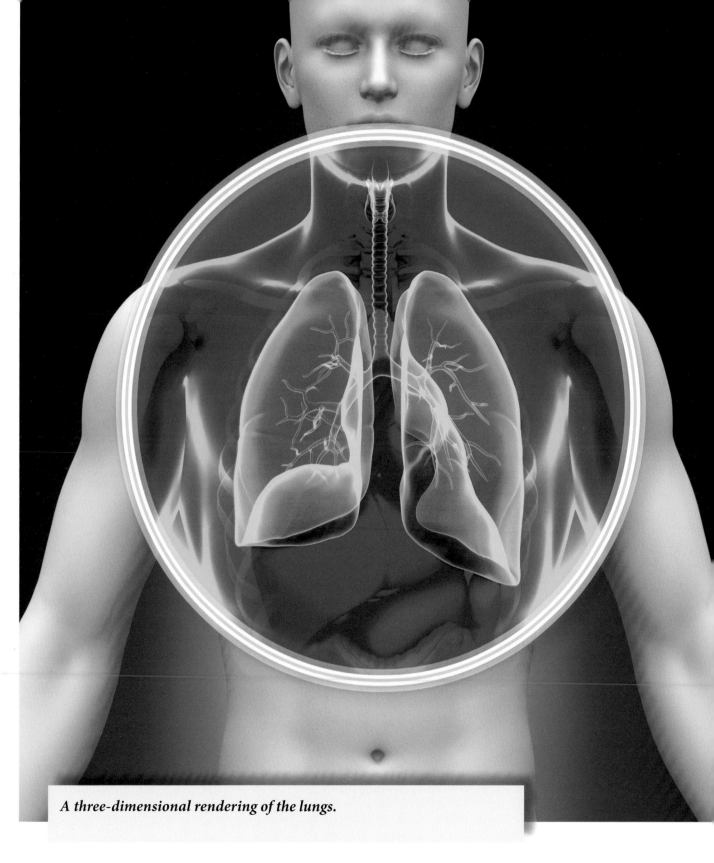

A three-dimensional rendering of the lungs.

although the embedded arsenic did lead to skin cancer years later. But that's what science, medicine, and research are all about: learning through trial and error. As it happens, one of Ronald Chodosh's relatives happened to be Jonas Salk, a famous researcher and physician who, in 1955, developed a vaccine to fight one of the world's most crippling disorders of the twentieth century: polio. How did he accomplish this laudable goal? Years of research, field tests, and trial and error.

But you don't have to have any treatments, injections, or field tests to learn about two of the most important workaholics in your body: your lungs.

Just take a deep breath…in, out… and read on.

CHAPTER ONE

OUR LUNGS

Our bodies are complicated, intricate, and sometimes quite baffling pieces of machinery. The body is so complex, in fact, that medical scientists and biologists—the folks who study it day in and day out—still don't know everything about it. They have questions, for example, about how the brain deals with love. And they wonder why some people are more likely than others to develop certain diseases or excel at particular professions.

What scientists do know, however, is that without oxygen, no part of the body—not the brain, the heart, the legs, the arms, or anything else—would work. More than anything else, we need oxygen, which is found in nature as a component of air, to survive. With oxygen, the trillions of cells that make up the individual building blocks of the body can live. Without it, they die.

The process by which oxygen is supplied to all living cells is called respiration, and the body system that controls this process is called the respiratory system. The primary body organs used in respiration are the two lungs, but other body parts—including the brain, the wall of the chest, and several muscles—also play important roles.

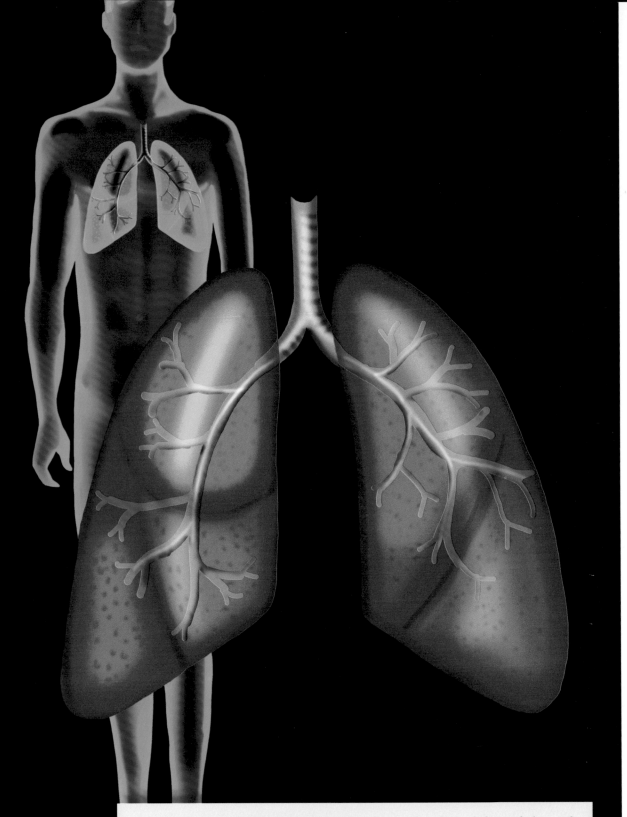

This illustration of the lungs clearly shows the three lobes of the right lung and the two lobes of the left lung.

A MAP OF THE LUNGS

The lungs themselves are quite ordinary looking. Light pink in color, at least initially, they are as big as organs go, but because they're full of air they weigh surprisingly little. They take up most of the space in the thoracic cavity, or chest, and because they come in pairs, they are conveniently referred to as "left" and "right." The left lung lies within the left half of the chest cavity, just to the left of the heart. The right lung is, as you might have guessed, to the right, just to the right of the heart. The heart itself, and the major blood vessels that connect to it, is separated from the lungs by a thin bag of protective tissue called the mediastinum.

Each lung is divided into visible lobes, or sections, by deep, rounded grooves called fissures. The right lung has three lobes, while the left has only two. Anatomists like to refer to the superior (toward the head) part of each lung, where it's at its narrowest, as the apex. The apex is located just behind the clavicle, which you probably know as the collarbone. The flat inferior (toward the feet) side of the lung is referred to as the base. The base sits on the diaphragm, an important muscle used in breathing.

Surrounding the lungs on their outer surfaces are two layers of wax-paper-like tissue called pleurae. The innermost layer of tissue, which attaches to the lungs, is known as the visceral pleura. The outside layer, which lines the internal chest walls, is called the parietal pleura. A narrow open region called the

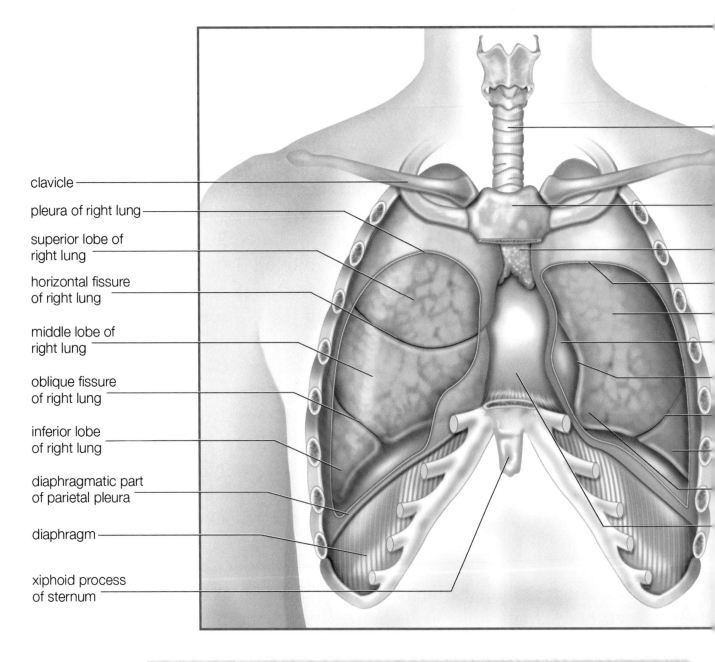

clavicle

pleura of right lung

superior lobe of
right lung

horizontal fissure
of right lung

middle lobe of
right lung

oblique fissure
of right lung

inferior lobe
of right lung

diaphragmatic part
of parietal pleura

diaphragm

xiphoid process
of sternum

A very detailed illustration of the lungs. Do you know what curved bones are missing? (Answer: the last word in the glossary definition of "intercostal muscles," on page 53.)

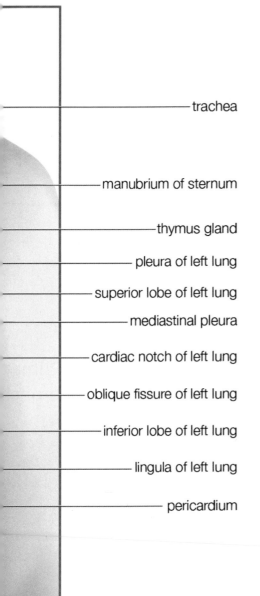

trachea

manubrium of sternum

thymus gland

pleura of left lung

superior lobe of left lung

mediastinal pleura

cardiac notch of left lung

oblique fissure of left lung

inferior lobe of left lung

lingula of left lung

pericardium

interpleural space separates the two pleural layers and is filled with a slippery fluid. The pleural fluid acts like a lubricant and allows the pleural layers to slip and slide back and forth over each other. At the same time, it causes the two layers to cling to one another, much like two panes of glass might "stick" together when wet. This means the lungs essentially cling to the internal walls of the chest, so when your chest expands, like when you begin to take a breath of air, your lungs expand, too.

THE ROUTE TO RESPIRATION

To understand the inside of the lungs, it helps to know a little about how they connect to the outside world. Respiration is made possible by the act of breathing. When we breathe, we pull air, and the oxygen that's in it, down a series of passageways that lead to the lungs. These passageways serve several

The Respiratory System

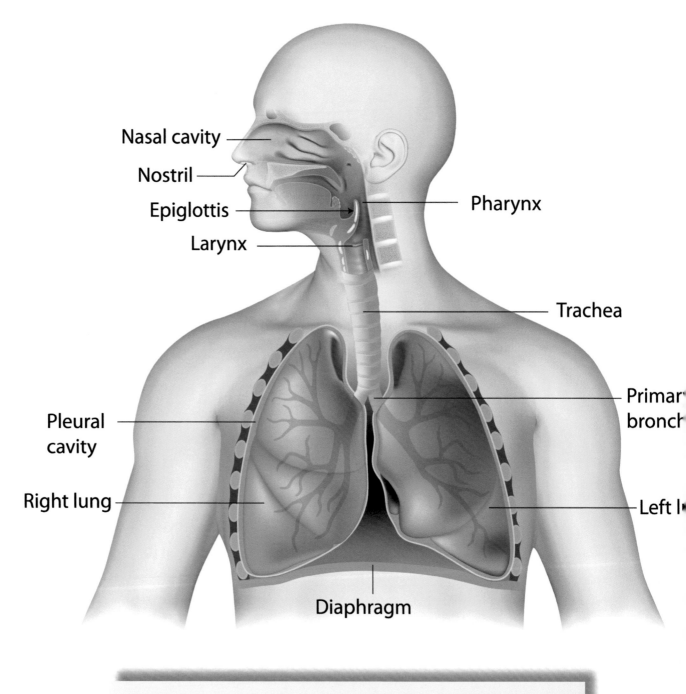

Nasal cavity

Nostril

Epiglottis

Larynx

Pharynx

Trachea

Primar bronch

Pleural cavity

Right lung

Left l

Diaphragm

Whether you breathe in through your nose, mouth, or both, the air will find its way down your pharynx (throat), which is the first step in the respiratory cycle.

purposes: to direct the air to the lungs and to filter, moisten, and warm the air before it gets there.

You're probably well acquainted with the first two passageways. The nose and the mouth are the entrance points for air. Air enters the nose through the nostrils, which anatomists like to call the "external nares." Beyond the nostrils is the nasal cavity. The walls of the nasal cavity are lined with mucous membranes. Glands in the mucous membranes produce a sticky substance called mucus, which moistens the air as it passes by and traps much of the microscopic dirt and bacteria that is in it. Veins, which carry blood to the heart, branch like a web directly behind the mucous membranes. The warm blood in the veins acts like a heater for the nearby mucus, which in turn transfers some of that heat to the air as it passes by.

The nasal cavity is surrounded by a number of hollow spaces within the skull called sinuses. The sinuses serve several purposes. Because they're essentially empty chambers, they make the skull lighter. They also secrete more mucus, which leaks into the nasal cavities to join the mucus created there.

The passageway from the mouth and the nasal cavity is known as the pharynx, or throat. Both food from the mouth and air from the mouth or nose can travel down the pharynx. The pharynx has three main parts. The uppermost part is called the nasopharynx. This is the nasal connector—where air from the nasal cavity enters the pharynx. Below the nasopharynx is the oropharynx, the oral part of the pharynx. Air and food from the mouth travel through the oropharynx, as does air from the

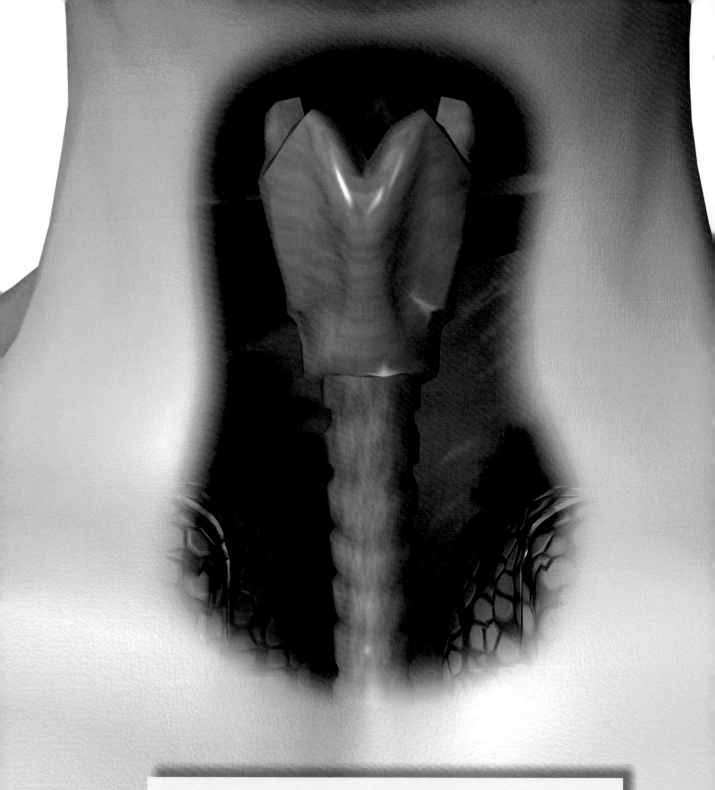

This "X-ray vision" illustration shows us the larynx. The shiny V-like protrusion of thyroid cartilage at the top of the larynx is often called the Adam's apple.

nose that has already passed through the nasopharynx. The last part of the pharynx, located below the oropharynx, is the laryngopharynx. The entire pharynx, including all three of its parts, is around 5 inches long (12.5 centimeters) in the average adult.

THE LARYNX:
VOICE BOX AND GATEKEEPER

Below and continuous with the pharynx is the larynx, or voice box. It's called the voice box because it houses the vocal cords, which are used in speaking. The larynx is formed by eight pieces of rigid cartilage, but its most obvious feature is the shield-like thyroid cartilage, or Adam's apple. The larynx is the "gatekeeper" for the remaining passageways to the lungs. Its main job, made possible by a flap of elastic cartilage at its top end called the epiglottis, is to make sure that only air—and not food or liquids—can enter. When you swallow, the larynx is pulled upward and the epiglottis tips to form a protective lid over its opening. When we're not swallowing and are just breathing, the epiglottis does not block the opening to the larynx. The lid forces food and liquids to travel down the esophagus toward the stomach and keeps them from going down the trachea, which is the main airway. If anything other than air does somehow make it into the larynx, a cough reflex usually forces it back up.

Air from the larynx travels down and into the trachea, or windpipe. The trachea is about 4 inches (10 cm) long in the

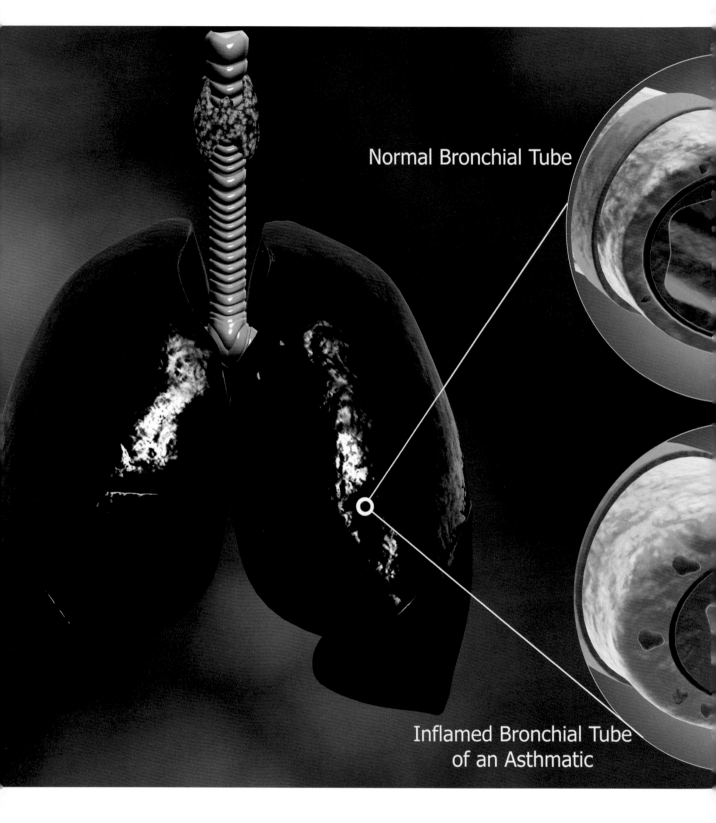

Normal Bronchial Tube

Inflamed Bronchial Tube
of an Asthmatic

average adult. Like the larynx, it's rigid and reinforced with C-shaped strips of cartilage, which you can feel when you tilt your head back and rub the ventral part (toward the front) of your neck. The open end of the C, on the dorsal side (toward the back) where there is no cartilage, borders the esophagus and allows the esophagus to expand when you swallow.

BRANCHING OUT TO THE BRONCHIOLES

At the bottom of the trachea, the airway branches into two major tubes called the left and right main bronchi. The right bronchus leads to the right lung. The left bronchus leads to left lung. Within the lungs, the bronchi branch into smaller and smaller bronchi. It's a lot like a main tree branch dividing into smaller branches. The smallest of the bronchi branches (like twigs) are called bronchioles.

The last of the air-conducting bronchioles are called terminal bronchioles. They, in turn, split into even smaller branches called respiratory bronchioles. The respiratory bronchioles eventually end at microscopic air sacs called alveoli, where gas exchange between the lungs and blood takes place. Scientists estimate that the average lung has around three hunded million alveoli.

What differences do you see in the two cross-sections shown here?

19

CHAPTER TWO

HOW WE BREATHE

You're reading now, concentrating on the words and the images, but your eyes and brain aren't the only organs at work. As discussed in the introduction, your lungs are doing their part, too, without any conscious effort from you. Want to focus on how you breathe? Close your eyes for a few moments and take several deep, cleansing breaths. Then open your eyes. That felt good, right? Relaxing. Do it again, feeling the air as it rushes down your throat and fills your lungs. Hold it there for a second. Now, release. Let the air pour out, all the way out. Let your body relax. OK. Now, stop. Don't breathe in. Just wait. How long did you last? If you're like most people, you probably were able to hold your breath for a few seconds. Then, because you absolutely had to—you didn't have a choice—you inhaled again.

YOUR BRAIN HAS YOU COVERED

Breathing is automatic. Because your body needs oxygen to survive, it also tells you when you have to breathe. In fact, it's

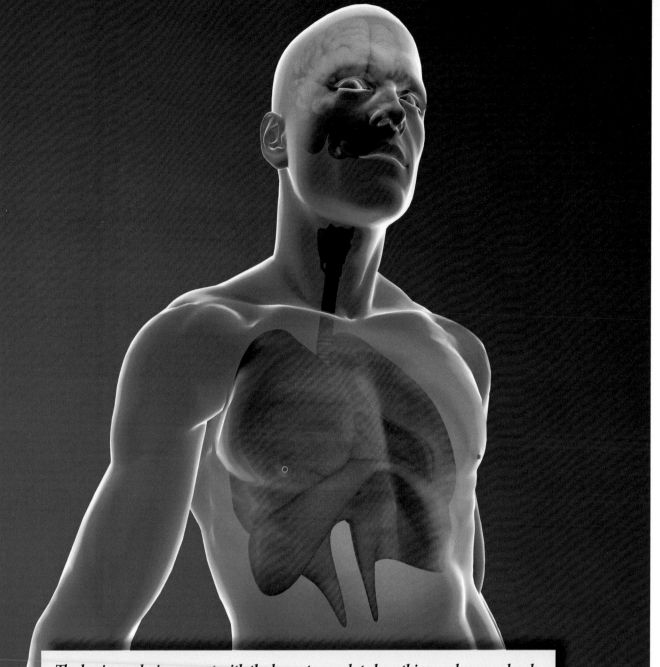

The brain works in concert with the lungs to regulate breathing and oxygen levels.

the brain that controls your basic breathing rhythm and how much air you take in with each breath. The brain receives signals from special receptors in the heart and the carotid artery (the big blood vessel in the neck) when oxygen levels in the blood begin to drop and when carbon dioxide levels begin to rise. In reply to those signals, the brain sends a separate message down the spinal cord to nerves that connect to the muscles of the respiratory system. When the muscles finally get the order, they immediately kick into gear and start the actual breathing process.

Inhalation, or "inspiration," as it's also known, is the first mechanical stage of the breathing process. It begins when the diaphragm, a narrow, dome-shaped muscle positioned immediately below the lungs, and the intercostal muscles, which are located between each rib, receive a message from the brain to contract. The diaphragm moves down from its normal resting position and flattens out near the bottom of the thoracic cavity, pushing on the lower ribs just enough to force them slightly out. At the same time, the intercostal muscles pull the upper ribs and sternum (the breastplate) in an upward and outward direction. It all sounds fairly complex, but the result is simple: the size of the chest increases.

GOOD GASSES

Because the lungs are essentially "stuck" to the inside chest wall by their pleural layers, when the chest expands it stretches the lungs out with it. And when this happens, all kinds of interesting things take place. For one, the gases contained in the lungs spread out to fill the bigger space, resulting in a decrease in pressure. The

The movements of the chest during breathing

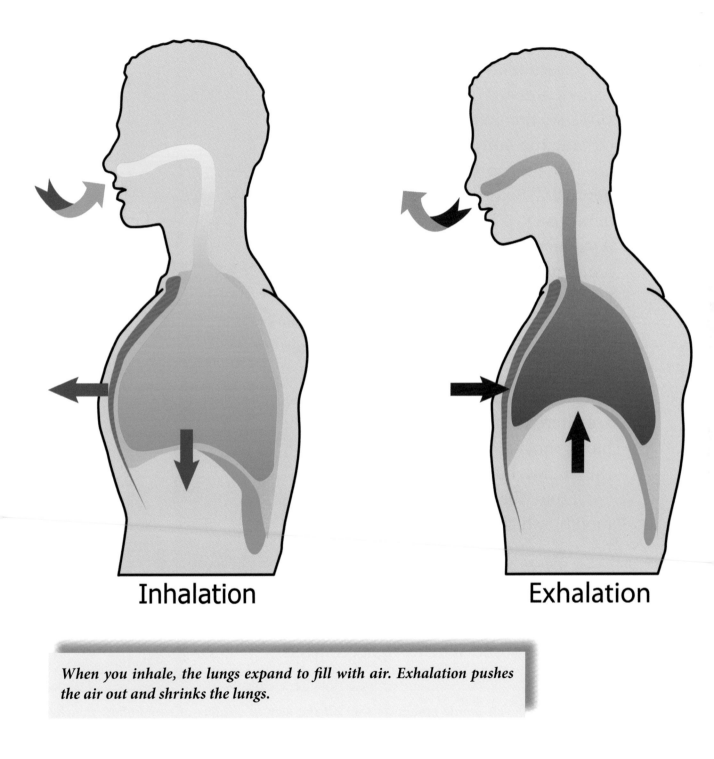

Inhalation

Exhalation

When you inhale, the lungs expand to fill with air. Exhalation pushes the air out and shrinks the lungs.

pressure decreases so much, in fact, that it quickly becomes lower than that of the air outside the body.

Gases tend to move from areas of higher pressure to areas of lower pressure, so the higher-pressure air from outside the body—especially that right around the nose and mouth—is suddenly drawn into the body, a lot like dirt being sucked in by a vacuum cleaner. Air, and whatever else is in it—dust, pollen, smoke, small bugs, you name it—rushes in through the mouth and nose. There, in a split second, it's prepped for delivery to the lungs. Bugs and other large objects are snagged by nasal hairs or caught by the tongue. Soot and dust are filtered out by a sticky layer of warm, moist mucus. The air itself is, thanks to the mucus, heated and humidified.

From the back of the nose or the mouth (which one depends on how you breathe—through your nose, your mouth, or both), the air continues down through the pharynx, is directed into the trachea, and splits left and right at the bronchi. The air that rushes into the right bronchus

Trachea

The air you inhale makes its way all the way to clusters of tiny hollow pouches called alveoli. (Alveolus is the singular form of the word.) In the pages to come you'll discover what these little grapelike sacs do.

HUMAN LUNG

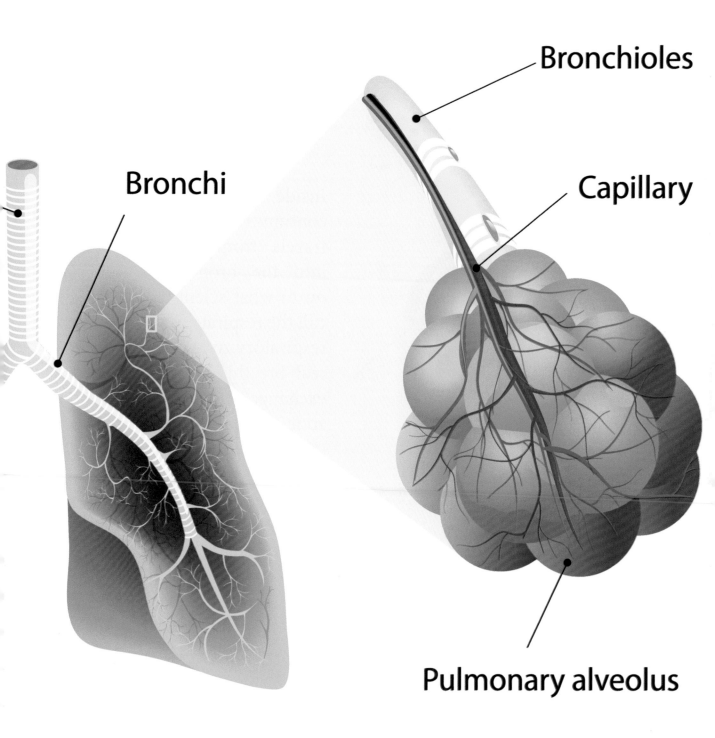

Bronchi

Bronchioles

Capillary

Pulmonary alveolus

heads to the right lung, while that in the left bronchus heads for the left lung.

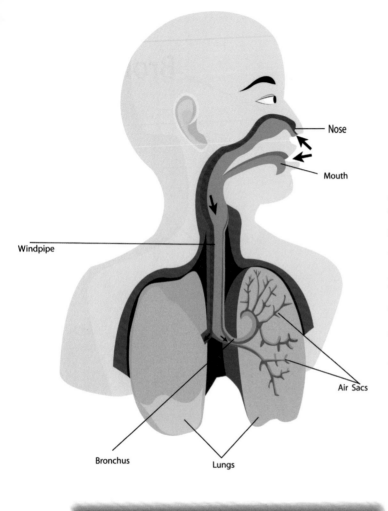

Nose

Mouth

Windpipe

Air Sacs

Bronchus

Lungs

Human lungs are filled with the air sacs (alveoli) noted in this illustration. How filled? The average adult lung has three hundred million, so that is six hundred million total.

YOU'VE JUST ENTERED THE RESPIRATORY ZONE

Inside each lung, the air continues on its way. It travels from the bronchi, into the bronchioles, and on to what scientists like to call the respiratory zone. The respiratory zone is where the real breathing process—gas exchange—takes place. The zone includes narrow passageways called respiratory bronchioles; alveolar ducts, which act like connecting pipes to alveolar sacs; and alveolar sacs, which anchor clusters of tiny, hollow, grape-like alveoli. Gas exchange (for a description

REGULAR RESPIRATION

You can tell how your breathing is going by counting the number of times you breathe every minute. Most healthy adults, when they're not exercising, take twelve to twenty breaths per minute. Children tend to breathe more, around fifteen to thirty times per minute. Infants breathe most often. Their normal range is anywhere from twenty-five to fifty breaths per minute. When you watch a person breathe, you can see his or her chest expand with every inhalation and shrink with every exhalation. Count one inhalation plus one exhalation as one full breath. Many factors can influence respiration, and what is normal for one person may not be normal for the next. Your size, sex, age, and physical conditioning all play important roles in how often you breathe.

of the process, see the next section), during which oxygen enters the bloodstream and carbon dioxide and other waste gases enter the lungs, occurs through the extremely thin walls of the alveoli.

NOW LET IT ALL OUT

At the very end of the inhalation process, when your lungs "feel full," the pressure within them is equal to the pressure of air in the atmosphere outside of the body. When this state occurs, the respiratory muscles, their job done, start to relax. Exhalation, or expiration, begins.

The exhalation process is the opposite of inhalation. The diaphragm moves up, and the ribs and sternum move down and back to their normal resting positions, decreasing the size of the thoracic cavity. As the chest space narrows, so does the space within the lungs. Eventually, because of the squeezing, the pressure of the gases in the lungs rises to a point that is higher than the atmospheric pressure outside the body. Then, because gases tend to move from areas of higher pressure to areas of lower pressure, the higher-pressure gas inside the lungs is forced out of the body. Up and out it goes, retracing—in reverse—the exact same route the air took on the way in.

Even after complete exhalation, a small amount of air remains in the lungs. You can try all you want to "blow" this air out of your body, but you won't succeed. Why? Well, the answer has to do with the body's need for a continuous supply of oxygen. If you were to get rid of all the air in your lungs, gas exchange

An artist's rendering of human lungs, bronchi, and trachea.

could no longer take place and oxygen would not make it to the cells. And that, of course, could prove deadly. This extra, "residual volume" of air essentially allows your body to continue breathing between actual breaths.

IT'S ALL NATURAL

As you can see, the breathing process is mostly beyond our conscious control. But we can influence breathing to some extent. Remember when you tried to keep from inhaling at the beginning of this section? You were able to delay breathing for at most a few seconds. When you "hold" your breath, that's exactly what you're doing: putting the breathing process on temporary hold. You also influence your breathing, whether intentionally or not, when you talk, cough, sneeze, hiccup, or exercise. Think about it—the last time you ran as fast as you could go, what was your breathing like when you finally stopped?

Still, when it comes to breathing, there's no doubt who's in charge: your body, and your respiratory system in particular. So the next time you find yourself thinking about your breathing, relax. Let nature do its job.

CHAPTER THREE

A VITAL PARTNERSHIP: OUR HEART AND LUNGS

Although the heart—a muscular, fist-sized organ that pumps blood throughout your body—is the star of the cardiovascular system, it is also a central, essential figure in your respiratory system. It is, in fact, located between your lungs, acting as your own personal blood pump. Through regular, well-timed contractions of its various components, it sends blood to every part of your body.

WHERE SHALL WE START?
THE BLOOD AND THE HEART

Not surprisingly, the incredibly important job of the respiratory system—to supply the entire body with the oxygen it needs to survive—would be absolutely impossible without blood and the heart. You can think of blood as a liquid taxicab. It picks up oxygen from the lungs, drives through the heart, and then zooms away to the rest of the body, dropping off enough oxygen at each cell to sustain life. Meanwhile, it picks up carbon dioxide and other "waste products" that you don't need and drives them to the lungs, where they can be exhaled out of the body.

The heart's job in this process is to pump the blood where it needs to go. But to understand truly how the heart works, you must also know how it's built. The heart has two main divisions, right and left, and consists of four major chambers,

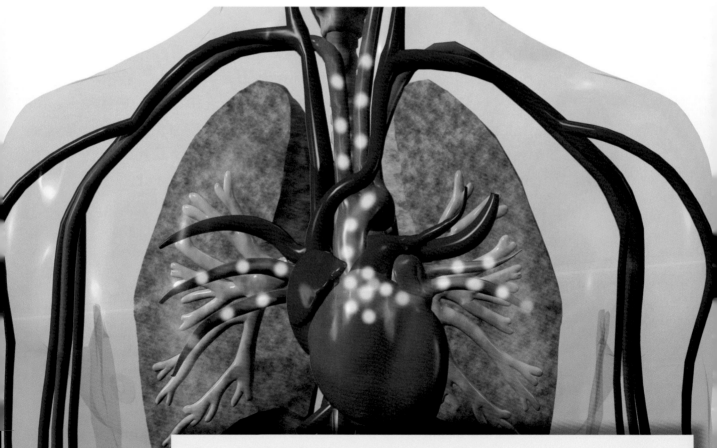

These white bubbles represent the oxygen that blood transports to the heart and beyond.

two on the right and two on the left. The upper chambers on each side of the heart are called the atria. The lower chambers are known as ventricles. The muscle-bound chambers, through which all blood flows, do the actual pumping.

The pathway of blood flow through the heart

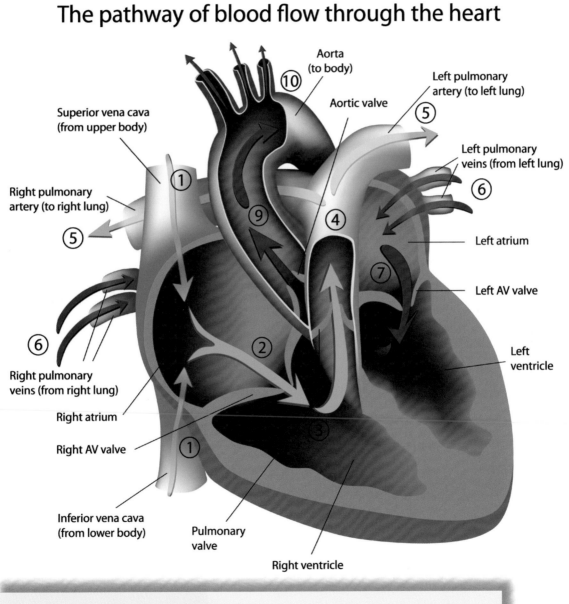

Blood flows through your heart following a very specific path, moved along by the pumping action of its chambers.

PUMPING YOU UP!

Here's how it works: blood low in oxygen but high in carbon dioxide enters the heart at the right atrium through big blood vessels called venae cavae. This blood contains very little oxygen because it dumped off most of it at the body's cells. It also holds lots of carbon dioxide because carbon dioxide is a natural by-product of metabolism, the process by which cells use oxygen to convert food into energy. The deoxygenated blood is pumped down and into the right ventricle through a one-way valve, then out of the heart and to the lungs through a major vessel called the pulmonary artery. The pulmonary artery is the only artery in the body that carries deoxygenated blood. As the pulmonary artery enters the lungs, it branches into smaller vessels called arterioles. Finally, it branches again, this time into even smaller blood vessels known as capillaries. The capillaries are microscopically thin—so thin, in fact, that they're perfect for gas exchange. In the lungs, they drape like webs over the alveoli.

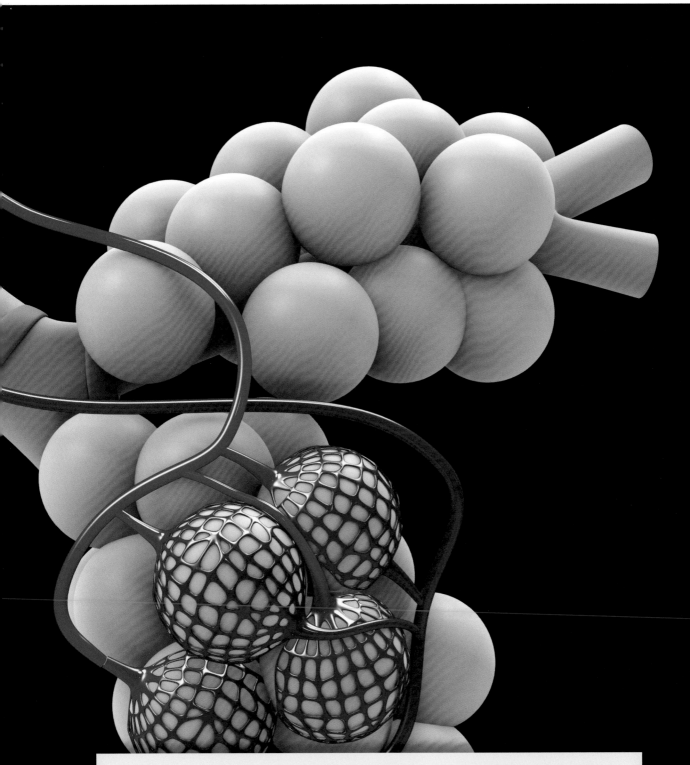

Alveoli, four of which are shown encased within the netting of ultra-thin capillaries. The red blood is oxygen-rich; blue lines show blood that needs to be re-oxygenated.

ALVEOLUS GAS EXCHANGE

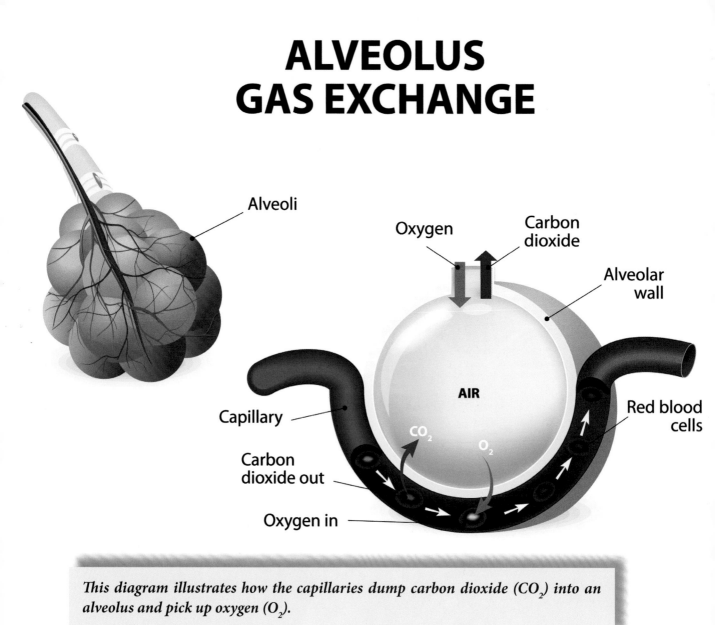

This diagram illustrates how the capillaries dump carbon dioxide (CO_2) into an alveolus and pick up oxygen (O_2).

Gas exchange in the lungs, called external respiration or pulmonary gas exchange, involves the actual swapping of gases between the alveoli and the blood. As you know, during inspiration, oxygen-rich air enters and fills the millions of alveoli scattered throughout the lungs. But the oxygen does the body no good when it's stuck inside the alveoli. For it to be of any use, it must be transferred to the blood and transported to the rest of the body. And that's where the capillaries come into play.

Remember—the blood in the capillaries is very low in oxygen and very high in carbon dioxide. And the air in the alveoli is high in oxygen and low in carbon dioxide. Because gases tend to move from areas of high concentration to areas of low concentration, this setup proves perfect for a swap. Oxygen in the alveoli passes through the thin capillary walls and into the bloodstream, where it hitches a ride by attaching to special molecules called hemoglobin. At the same time, carbon dioxide leaves the capillaries and enters the alveoli. The blood in the capillaries, which is now rich with oxygen, continues on its way. And upon exhalation the carbon dioxide in the alveoli is ejected out of the body and into the air.

The newly oxygenated blood now heads back to the heart. The capillaries merge into larger vessels called venules, the venules lead to pulmonary veins, and the pulmonary veins enter the heart at the left atrium. The heart's job at this point is simple: send the oxygen-rich blood out to all the body's cells. Wasting no time, it directs the blood down into the left ventricle through another one-way valve, and with a swift, muscular contraction, pumps it out of the heart through the aortic artery.

THE ART AND SCIENCE OF ARTERIES

The aorta is the heart's main artery. It supplies all other arteries in the body with high-oxygen blood. Those arteries include

Oxygen Transport Cycle

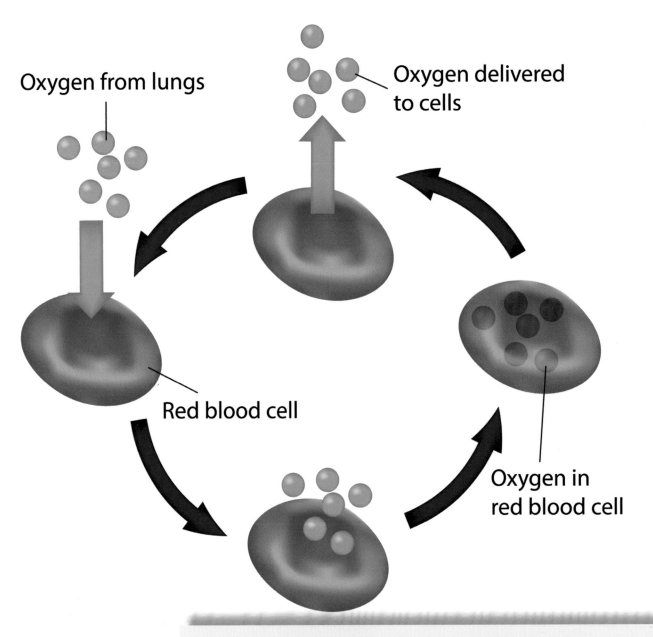

Oxygen from lungs

Oxygen delivered to cells

Red blood cell

Oxygen in red blood cell

When we breathe in, oxygen-rich blood cells flow through the lungs. After depositing that oxygen, those cells, now filled with carbon dioxide, travel back up where they can release the CO_2 and load up on oxygen once again. And so on and so on.

CO_2: A GIFT FROM YOU!

You may wonder just what happens to all the carbon dioxide that you expel into the air every time you exhale. Fortunately, at least some of it is put to use. In fact, plants love it. Plants absorb carbon dioxide from the air in a process called photosynthesis. With the aid of sunlight and water, special molecules in plants called chlorophyll convert carbon dioxide into useful compounds that are essential for growth. So the next time you find yourself breathing with nothing else to do, stroll on over to a houseplant and give it CO_2!

the coronary arteries, which give the heart its blood supply; the carotid arteries, which lead up the neck and to the head and brain; the femoral arteries, which are in the thighs and legs; the brachial arteries, in the upper arms; and the radial arteries, in the lower arms. Other arteries lead elsewhere in the body. You can feel blood as it squeezes through the arteries when you take a pulse. Try checking your own radial pulse by placing three fingers on the palm-side of your wrist, right beneath your thumb.

The arteries eventually branch into smaller arterioles, then branch again into capillaries, which are found in every part of the body. At this point, another episode of gas exchange must take place in order to send oxygen out of the blood and into the body's cells. This swap, known as internal respiration, is the

This 3D ultrasound scan of a human heart shows the coronary arteries and the smaller, tributary-like arterioles.

gas-exchange process that occurs between the capillaries and the cells that they cover.

Again, similar to the process that takes place in the lungs, the gas exchange is fairly straightforward. Only this time the tables are reversed. In internal respiration, the blood in the capillaries surrounding the body's cells is full of oxygen that it picked up from the lungs but very low in carbon dioxide. The cells, on the other hand, are loaded with carbon dioxide but lacking oxygen. The gases, as usual, do their little dance and move from areas of high concentration to areas of low concentration. Oxygen passes through the thin capillary membrane and into the cells, while carbon dioxide steps out of the cells and into the capillary blood stream.

The blood, now high in carbon dioxide and low in oxygen, travels from the capillaries to larger venules, from venules to larger veins, into the venae cavae, and back into the heart. The heart, of course, directs the blood into the pulmonary vein and out to the lungs to start the whole process over again.

CHAPTER FOUR

METABOLIZING OXYGEN

We all use energy every day—whether we're snowboarding or sleeping, bicycling uphill, or just breathing in bed. Even if you're lying perfectly still, you need energy to pump the blood in your heart all the way down your body and into your toes. Energy is vital for every single aspect of life.

Fortunately, if you like to eat, energy is not exactly hard to come by. You get your energy from food—everything from pasta to chicken to fish to fruits and vegetables. You might wonder just how it is that the human body is able to take something as basic as a piece of pie and turn it into something useful, like the energy to hammer a nail or lift a heavy book. The answer has to do with a complicated chemical process called metabolism.

EAT UP; CHOW DOWN: THE NUTRIENTS ARE GOING TO TOWN

The conversion of food into usable energy begins with digestion, when most nutrients are absorbed into the bloodstream through the intestines and into the intestinal capillaries. Once the nutrients enter the bloodstream, a vein carries them to the liver. From there the nutrients are transported to cells throughout the body. Cells pick up the nutrients in almost the same way they accumulate oxygen. The nutrients move from areas of higher concentration in the blood to areas of low concentration in the cells. Once the nutrients are in the cells, the metabolic process begins.

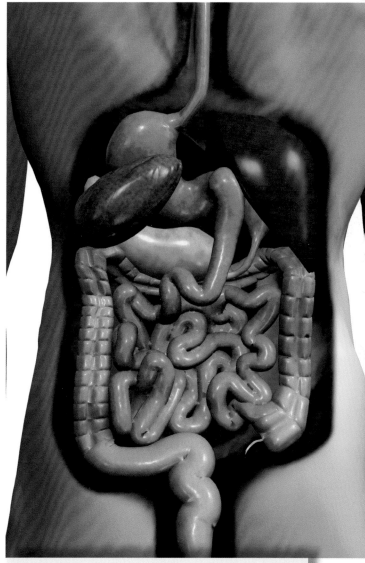

The human digestive system, from the stomach (pink) and the liver (brown) at the top, to the rectum at the bottom.

The word "metabolism," when used in science, refers to all the chemical and energy changes that occur in the body. More specifically, it refers to the ability of the body's cell's to take oxygen from the lungs and use it to help convert carbohydrates, fat, and protein from food into the high-energy chemical compound ATP, or adenosine triphosphate. When a food item as simple as a potato, for example, is eaten, digested, delivered to the body's cells as nutrients, and then combined with oxygen (oxidized) to make ATP, those cells can take that energy and use it immediately to do work.

Oxidation of food nutrients and the production of ATP occur only in specialized cellular parts called mitochondria. Some cells have more mitochondria than others. The more mitochondria a cell has, the greater its ability to produce ATP.

THE TIME FACTOR

The rate at which our cells metabolize food is what determines how much oxygen those cells need. When we're sitting

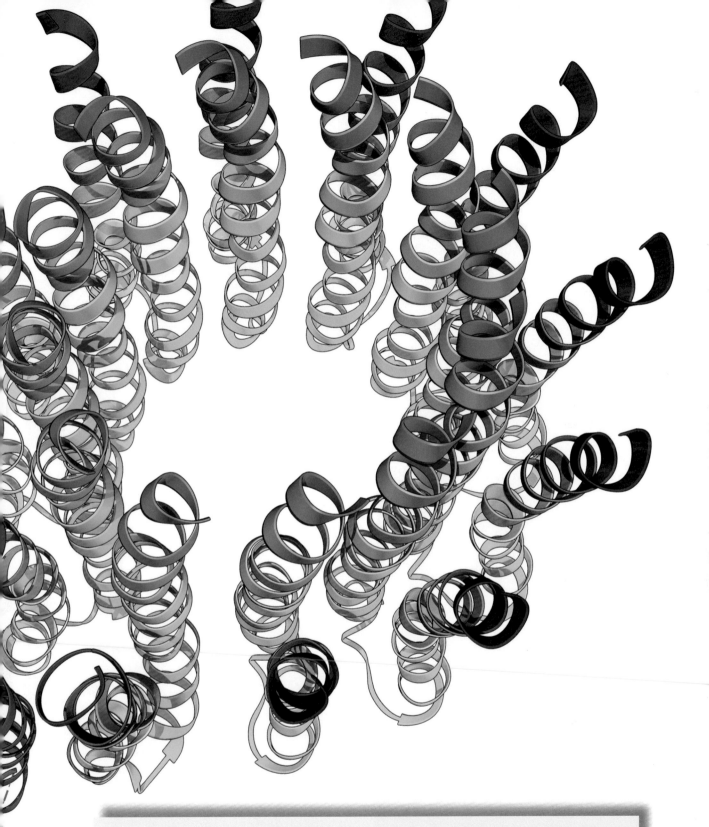

Model of an adenosine triphosphate (ATP) molecule. Filled with energy (which is obtained from the breakdown of foods), these molecules are found in all living cells.

around doing nothing or sleeping, the oxygen needs of our cells are at their lowest. At times like this, our blood can easily deliver enough oxygen to the cells for metabolism to

FEELING WINDED?

If you've ever wondered why you breathe so hard when you're running or biking up a hill, now you know why. You're burning through your ATP, and your cells are begging for oxygen so they can make more. By breathing harder—an act that you cannot control in this instance—your body is taking in more air and sending the oxygen from that air to your muscles.

A similar thing happens at high altitudes. Because there is less oxygen in the air at high altitudes, people who live at sea level and travel to places above 7,000 feet (2,134 meters) often find themselves out of breath every time they move. Again, their bodies are telling them they need more

Sometimes during a challenging game of soccer (or any active sport), you need to take a breather and restore some much-needed oxygen to your body.

oxygen for metabolism and are forcing them to breathe more air as a result.

Of course, in both of these examples it's not hard to overcome the need to breathe hard. All you have to do is train your body. In the case of problems breathing at high altitudes, the best plan of attack is gradual acclimatization. When you acclimatize, you spend enough time at high altitude to allow your body to adjust to the low oxygen levels. When you do so, your body naturally develops more

(continued on the next page)

Oxygenated red blood cells, rushing to where they're needed.

(continued from the previous page)

and more red blood cells—the cells that carry oxygen. This increases your body's ability to take in and transport oxygen to the muscles that need them.

When it comes to that hill, on the other hand, the best thing to do is get in shape. If you can build the specific muscles involved in running or biking, for example, you'll increase the amount of mitochondria within them. And the more mitochondria you have, the better your muscles will be at converting nutrients into energy. That said, don't beat yourself up if you're winded after having run back and forth across the soccer pitch or the basketball court several times. Even trained athletes get winded.

proceed. During exercise, however, when we're burning up our energy at a much faster rate, we need much more oxygen, ten to twenty times as much as that which we need at rest. The more work our muscles do, the more the cells in those muscles need additional ATP.

When your muscles are first used following rest, they hold enough ATP reserves to fuel activity for a few seconds. But once this ATP is used up, new ATP must be made. At first, chemicals in the bloodstream get additional ATP by breaking down a compound stored in the muscles called creatine phosphate. But again, after a few seconds of muscular activity, the supply runs out. At this point, the body must get ATP through metabolism.

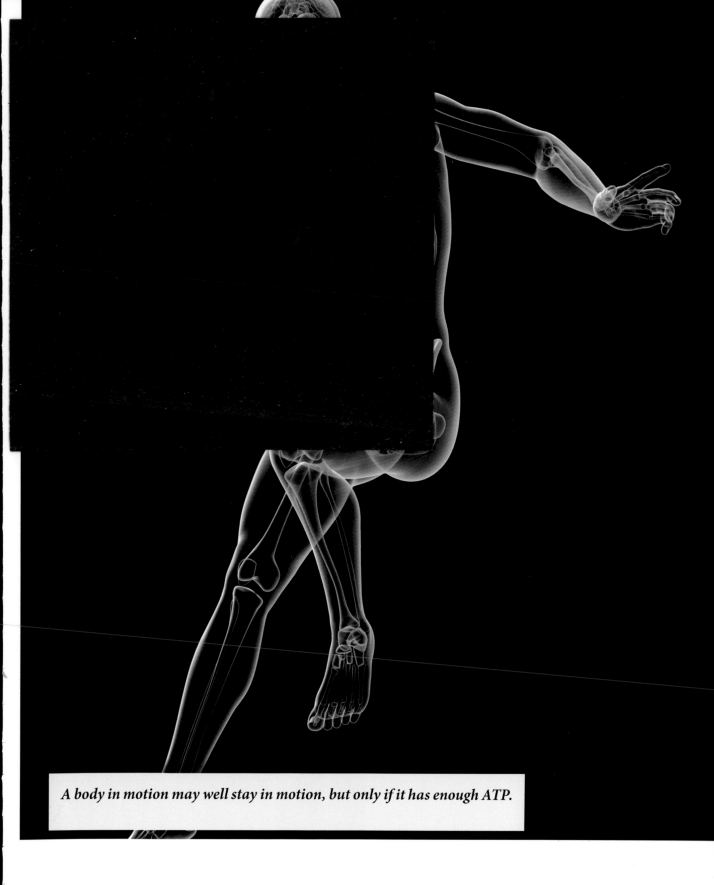

A body in motion may well stay in motion, but only if it has enough ATP.

BURN NOTICE

Highly conditioned athletes can train their respiratory and cardiovascular systems to take in and use oxygen at extremely high rates—much higher than the average couch potato. Still, as noted earlier, even the best athletes eventually reach a point where their oxygen intake is not enough to satisfy their metabolic needs. This can happen for a number of reasons, including the inability of the heart to pump an adequate amount of blood at a rate fast enough to deliver oxygen to the muscles that need it. When this happens, metabolism becomes anaerobic—that is, it occurs without oxygen. Anaerobic metabolism is not nearly as efficient as aerobic metabolism in converting food

A transmitted light micrograph (where the object viewed is backlit) shows adenosine triphosphate in extreme detail.

compounds into energy. The result of anaerobic metabolism is that waste products from the metabolic process accumulate in the bloodstream. Eventually the waste products, especially lactic acid, limit the athlete's ability to use his or her muscles. If you've ever felt a severe burning feeling in your legs from running very fast for a long period of time or hiking or biking up a steep hill, you know exactly what lactic acid feels like.

Aerobic metabolism also results in waste products, especially carbon dioxide and water. But unlike lactic acid, carbon dioxide and water are both easily eliminated from the body when we exhale.

And so whether you've been running or reading, cycling or eating, once again take a deep breath… in, out… and thank your circulatory system, your heart, and that stalwart duo, your lungs.

GLOSSARY

ANATOMY The study of the structure of the body and all of its parts.

ATMOSPHERIC PRESSURE The pressure of air outside the body.

BLOOD VESSELS Arteries, veins, capillaries, and other pipelike parts of the body used in the circulation of blood.

CARBON DIOXIDE A naturally occurring gas that is a by-product of metabolism.

DEOXYGENATED BLOOD Blood that is low in or lacking oxygen.

EXHALATION Breathing out; expiration.

EXTERNAL RESPIRATION The gas-exchange process that occurs between capillaries and the alveoli in the lungs.

GAS EXCHANGE The process by which two or more gases change places.

INHALATION Breathing in; inspiration.

INTERCOSTAL MUSCLES Muscles located between each rib.

INTERNAL RESPIRATION The gas-exchange process that occurs between capillaries and the body's cells.

INTERPLEURAL SPACE The space between pleural layers in the lungs.

MEMBRANE A thin layer of body tissue.

METABOLISM The chemical changes in cells that produce energy necessary for life.

OXYGEN A naturally occurring gas found in air that is vital for all life.

OXYGENATED BLOOD Blood that has oxygen in it.

PARIETAL PLEURA A layer of tissue that lines the internal chest walls.

PULMONARY ARTERY The artery in the body that carries oxygenated blood from the heart to the lungs.

RESPIRATION The process by which oxygen and carbon dioxide are exchanged during breathing.

RESPIRATORY SYSTEM The organs in the body involved in breathing.

RESPIRATORY ZONE The parts of the respiratory system including the respiratory bronchioles, alveolar ducts, alveolar sacs, and alveoli.

THORACIC CAVITY The chest.

VISCERAL PLEURA A layer of tissue that attaches to the lungs.

FOR MORE INFORMATION

American Association of Anatomists

9650 Rockville Pike

Bethesda, MD 20814-3998

(301) 634-7910

Website: http://www.anatomy.org

The American Association of Anatomists was founded in 1888 for the "advancement of anatomical science." Today, via research, education, and professional development activities, AAA serves as the professional home for an international community of biomedical researchers and educators focusing on the structural foundation of health and disease.

American Lung Association

55 W. Wacker Drive, Suite 1150

Chicago, IL 60601

(800) LUNGUSA (Call this number to contact the American Lung Association nearest you.)

(800) 548-8252 (Call this number to speak to a lung health professional at the HelpLine.)

(312) 801-7630 (Call this number for the National Office of the American Lung Association.)

Website: http://www.lungusa.org

The American Lung Association is a great source of information on lung disease, disease prevention, healthy air, and assistance for quitting smoking.

American Medical Association (AMA)

AMA Plaza

330 N. Wabash Avenue

Chicago, IL 60611

(800) 621-8335

Website: http://www.ama-assn.org

The American Medical Association aims to improve health care and medical education in the United States through the work of physicians.

The Canadian Lung Association

1750 Courtwood Crescent, Suite 300

Ottawa, ON K2C 2B5

Canada

(888) 566-5864

Website: http://www.lung.ca

The Canadian Lung Association fights for healthy lungs and clean air in Canada through research, advocacy, and education.

Centers for Disease Control and Prevention

1600 Clifton Road

Atlanta, GA 30329-4027

800-CDC-INFO (800-232-4636)

Website: http://www.cdc.gov

The CDC works to protect America from health, safety, and security threats, both foreign and in the United States. The CDC fights disease and supports communities and citizens to do the same. As the nation's health protection agency, the CDC saves lives and protects people from health threats. To accomplish its mission, the CDC conducts critical research and provides health information that protects our nation against expensive and dangerous health threats, and responds when these arise.

LungCancer.org

275 Seventh Avenue

22nd Floor

New York, NY 10001

800-813-HOPE (4673)

Website: http://www.lungcancer.org

LungCancer.org was founded in 1998 by CancerCare, a national nonprofit organization providing free, professional support services to individuals, families, caregivers, and the bereaved to help them better cope with and manage the emotional and practical challenges arising from cancer. The main purpose of

LungCancer.org is to be a source of support and information for lung cancer patients and their loved ones.

Lung Cancer Alliance

888 16th Street NW

Suite 150

Washington, DC 20006

(202) 463-2080

Lung Cancer Information Line: (800) 298-2436

Website: http://www.lungcanceralliance.org

Lung Cancer Alliance is the oldest and leading nonprofit organization dedicated to saving lives and advancing research by empowering those living with and at risk for lung cancer. Its mission is to save lives and advance research by empowering those living with or at risk for lung cancer.

National Heart, Lung, and Blood Institute (NHLBI)

National Institutes of Health

Building 31, Room 5A52

31 Center Drive MSC 2486

Bethesda, MD 20892

(301) 592-8573

Website: http://www.nhlbi.nih.gov

The National Institutes of Health is the U.S. Department of Health and Human Services' main agency for medical research and one of the world's most important research centers. The NHLBI works with patients, families, scientists, and physicians to conduct research on heart, lung, and blood diseases.

National Lung Health Education Program (NLHEP)

18000 West 105th Street

Olathe, KS 66061

(913) 895-4631

Website: http://www.nlhep.org/Pages/default.aspx

The National Lung Health Education Program (NLHEP) was developed in 1996 as a new health care initiative designed to increase awareness of chronic obstructive pulmonary disease (COPD) among the public and health care professionals and to encourage the use of simple spirometry to make an earlier diagnosis and monitor ongoing treatment.

WEBSITES

Because of the changing nature of Internet links, Rosen Publishing has developed an online list of websites related to the subject of this book. This site is updated regularly. Please use this link to access the list:

http://www.rosenlinks.com/HB3D/Lungs

FOR FURTHER READING

Amsel, Sheri. *The Everything Kids' Human Body Book*. Avon, MA: F+W Media, 2012.

DK. *Human Anatomy: The Definitive Visual Guide*. New York, NY: DK, 2014.

Figorito, Christine. *The Lungs in Your Body* (Let's Find Out! The Human Body). New York, NY: Britannica Educational Publishing, 2015.

Gold, Susan Dudley. *Learning About the Respiratory System* (Learning About the Human Body Systems). Berkeley Heights, NJ: Enslow Publishers, 2013.

Harmon, Daniel E. *Pollution and Your Lungs* (Incredibly Disgusting Environments). New York, NY: Rosen Publishing, 2013.

Jango-Cohen, Judith. *Your Respiratory System* (Searchlight Books: How Does Your Body Work?). Minneapolis, MN: Lerner Publishing, 2013.

McKinley, Michael, et al. *Human Anatomy*. 4th ed. New York, NY: McGraw-Hill Science/Engineering/Math, 2014.

Netter, Frank H. *Atlas of Human Anatomy*. 6th ed. Philadelphia, PA: Saunders, 2014.

Norris, Maggie, and Donna Rae Siegfried. *Anatomy and Physiology for Dummies*. Hoboken, NJ: Wiley Publishing, Inc., 2011.

Parker, Steve. *Super Human Encyclopedia: Discover the Amazing Things Your Body Can Do*. London, England: DK Publishing, 2014.

Roberts, Alice. *The Complete Human Body: The Definitive Visual Guide*. New York, NY: DK, 2010.

Simon, Seymour. *Lungs: All About Our Respiratory System and More!* New York, NY: HarperCollins, 2007.

Taylor-Butler, Christine. *The Respiratory System*. New York, NY: Scholastic, 2008.

Waldron, Melanie. *Your Respiration and Circulation: Understand Them with Numbers* (Your Body by Numbers). Hampshire, England: Raintree, 2014.

Williams, Ben. *Look Inside: Your Heart and Lungs*. Huntington Beach, CA: Teacher Created Materials, 2011.

INDEX

ABOUT THE AUTHORS

Although she did not follow in her father's professional footsteps as he had so dearly wanted—namely, becoming a physician—writer, editor, and photographer Hope Lourie Killcoyne has nonetheless enjoyed writing and editing medical-based books, such as this one.

Chris Hayhurst, an EMT, is a professional author and journalist with more than a dozen books and hundreds of articles in print. He lives and works in Fort Collins, Colorado.

PHOTO CREDITS